planting gardens in graves III

planting gardens in graves III

r.h. Sin

Andrews McMeel
PUBLISHING®

here with you.

i'm sorry for all the times
your screams went unheard
i'm sorry for all the moments
where you felt like
you were alone and no one cared
i'm sorry that your innocence
was stolen by the hands
of an abuser who claimed to love you
i'm sorry that your self-esteem
was shattered by the mouth
of someone
who instead of building you up
chose to tear down
the skyscraper in your soul
i'm sorry they left you behind
after promising to stay

i'm sorry that forever
has never been long enough
i'm sorry that your eyes
have been drowning in the ocean
of your own emotions
i'm sorry that your heart

doesn't know what it means
to be held in the hands
of someone who truly cares for it
i'm sorry that your efforts to fight
for something
haven't been met with victory
oftentimes you've been forced
to go into battle alone
i'm sorry that your soul
has struggled to find its mate

i'm sorry that you feel
this weight of the world
on your shoulders
i'm sorry and maybe this isn't enough
maybe my words will flow
through you
like an untouched river
maybe you'll see meaning
in these words
but only after you've finished
reading the pages in this book
maybe you just need time
maybe you just need a moment
to yourself
a space just for you
alone with your problems

a place where you can truly
come face to face with everything
that has happened
regardless of what you choose
to do
regardless of where you choose
to go
i believe in you
i believe in your ability
to calm your own storms
i believe in your ability
to put out the flames
that have burned you
for far too long

strangers we know.

silently we drown
reaching for the same hands
that pushed us into the sea
expecting the ones who broke us
to help us feel complete

yelling out their names
as they watch us go under
strangers in the fog
once upon a time
our lovers

new beginning.

there is new life
in letting go
there is a new beginning
in moving forward
you can't find love
where it doesn't exist
you'll never get
what you deserve
holding on to someone
who refuses
to love you completely

death and nothingness.

there is death

in holding on

nothingness

in refusing

to move forward

true love escapes

the hands of the lover

who latches on

to the ones

incapable of loving them back

always in waiting

hoping for the impossible

wasting away on a dream

that feels more like a nightmare

the strengthening.

most of our lessons
arrive in the form
of people who will
break our hearts
and even though it hurts
each heartbreak
makes us stronger

open your eyes and see.

this is the fucking issue

you're the only one fighting

for a relationship

that they gave up on

a long time ago

you can't save someone

who refuses to appreciate

your effort

you for you I.

you've always been selfless
but it's time to take care
of you now
it's okay to put yourself first
there's nothing wrong
with choosing yourself
when others refuse to choose you

your eyes only I.

to the girl reading this
in search of clarity and peace
tired of feeling broken
tired of feeling weak
i see you
i hear you
i understand

saying no.

stop giving to people
what they refuse
to give you

you for you II.

you are all you have
and lately, you've been everything
to yourself
but you are all you'll ever need

no rest.

your relationship drains you
and so sleeping does nothing
you wake up tired, your soul
is weary

strong from broken.

so many strong women
began as broken girls

your eyes only II.

this is for the girls
who are too tired to sleep
i know it's been difficult
i know it's been tough
but you are stronger than you know
you will find the peace
you deserve

<u>in time passing.</u>

years from now
he won't even matter
and everything he did to break you
will have only made you stronger

under many moons.

maybe she couldn't sleep
because she was made
for the night

women like her.

maybe
she just wants
to be loved madly

722 degrees.

this girl
could set fire
to the devil

several cracks.

the larger your heart
the more often
it gets broken

always never.

a woman

will never need

to chase after a man

who truly wants

to be a part of her life

January 13th 2007.

i had always thought that heartache

would never come for me

my ignorance was bliss

until the first time i was
introduced

to the very thing that would cause
me pain

a love that would later transform
into hate

hands that would go from causing

electricity beneath my skin

to leaving bruises, constant
reminders

of everything i would later regret

fooled by youthfulness

i fell as if i tripped with my shoes
untied

i found myself falling into a pit
of hell

that was labeled love

only, i didn't notice the signs until

it was too late

my heart placed in the hands of my
abuser

my whole life changed by one decision

a choice i made with blind eyes

as my mind lost all its ability

to act on logic

i followed my heart into a dark room

in search of something

that couldn't be seen

my faith invested on empty promises

but at the time, i had no idea

that I'd been believing the words
of a liar

everything's nicer in the beginning

it's the first time, so there's this
wonderful bliss

there's this feeling of floating

an unbelievable high like inhaling

the best herb

this is what i felt, i allowed myself
to feel this

i trusted the experience

because I'd never experienced it
before

the weeks turned into months

and the joy of it all

began to fade a little like a black
t-shirt

that's been washed way too many
times

starting over was like buying a
new shirt

only to watch it fade once more

then continuing the cycle

failing to realize that maybe that
t-shirt

wasn't made with the best quality

to begin with

our foundation slowly crumbling

like the colosseum in Rome

the type of destruction that
remodeling

couldn't fix

but there i stood in the middle of
it all

watching the walls of our colosseum

fall toward me

i would later lose years of my life

fighting for a love that was never
truly there

while grieving the death of my
teenage innocence

and everything else that had turned

into ashes

as the flames of betrayal continued

to burn down whatever was left

of whoever i was

so much energy

so much time

so much love

too much of everything

i gave but so much of it

treated as if it was never enough

i gave my all

but it was all for nothing

the first.

my first time was blurry

a pixelated mess

an unfortunate set of events

that would ruin my childhood
innocence

peer pressure and booze

too much to drink

too young to comprehend

too immature to think

it was nothing as i anticipated

sort of a fucked up situation

so many years ago

and still i wish i had waited

front center.

i've been sitting front row
to all of your lies
maintaining my silence
while aware of the truth
i see everything and say nothing
i should leave but i'm holding on
hoping for change
living in denial
in search of a love
you'll never provide

toward the future.

one day you won't matter

one day you'll just be a mistake

i made on the way to everything

that i've been searching

there will come a time

where this will no longer hurt

and you will no longer

have the power to dictate my
emotions

i look forward to the day

of realizing that losing you

meant dodging a bullet

remove pain.

i've been trying
to rid myself of you
crying in hopes of draining
out your existence
dipping the places you touched me
in bleach
but that never works

i set fire to our memories
watching as the flames
burned through all of our mementos
pieces of paper baring our names
notes written by you
filled with empty promises
and the lies i always believed
up until now

how i let myself stay here
beside you, hurting, neglected
in need of something
you were never willing to give
i now sit next to the bag of tricks
you fooled me with

i now sit here in my truth
chaos, misfortune, and hell
was loving you
and so I've been trying
to rid myself of you

left me behind.

i've been missing myself
i have no idea where i left me
lost in the bliss of ignorance
i abandoned the truth
for the arms of a liar
i abandoned myself
while trying to keep you

tune me out.

i wish

i hope

i pray

i'm silent

i speak up

i scream

i fight without being fought for

i try and it's never appreciated

in love but hating the relationship

that i'm in

taken but alone

next to you and yet i'm lonely

i am everything i never wanted
to be

and i have none of the things

that i believe i deserve

i'm silent and nothing changes

i speak up but everything remains
the same

i scream yet you never hear

because you don't care to listen

unheard, the pounding of my heart

unheard, the pain in my voice

the letdown.

winter grows within the soul
that knows what it means
to feel broken
let down by the very person
who promised a lifetime of love

nothing more.

you feel it
you feel so much
so much of what you feel
isn't reciprocated
and so you feel a bit more
you try harder
you make changes
you literally alter yourself
becoming the person
you believe they want
you feel for someone
who doesn't feel the same
you feel some more
until you just feel nothing

on edge.

there are moments
where life feels like a burden
i know this to be true
because life has often
been a bitch toward me

an inconsiderate bitch
with no appreciation
for how hard i try
i fight until i'm drained
by the hours in a day
stressed out by circumstance
broken by the loneliness
and frustration of it all

there are moments
where i'd like nothing more
but to clock out permanently
leaving behind my troubles
in hopes of finally resting in peace

i've been through it
more times than i can count
my body riddled with bruises
my mind on the edge, nearly falling
i've stared into the eyes of death
accepting of my would-be fate
as i create small talk with the reaper
no longer willing to bargain for my
soul

there are moments
where i want to give up
or give in to this urge
to lay down and let go
i too struggle just as much as you
but somehow i'm still fighting
we're still fighting

two strangers.

do you miss me yet
have i crossed your mind
are you cold without my warmth
do you feel the sting of my absence

i could've been
what i should've been
and now we'll never know
our relationship built upon pillars
of sand
i sat and watched
as the ocean washed it all away
everything became nothing
you and I, two strangers

where you touched me.

i wish my skin was a suit
i'd unzip it and change
to keep myself from
remembering you

love is blind.

there's a fog
covering my eyes
extending to my heart
my point of view, unclear
blinded, obstructed
i can't see what everyone else sees
and so i fall deeper than before
not knowing where i'll land
not knowing that you won't catch me

near day.

awake after midnight

three in the morning

and i'm restless

weary with the lovers

who feel lonely

under the same moon

broken, near daylight

waiting for the sun

on repeat.

sex doesn't keep people
they cum then go

more of this.

someone who loves me
for me and not for what i have
or what i can do for them
this love, this rare kind of love
is the type of love i crave
it's the type of love
that keeps me hoping for more

no going back.

your apologies
won't change my mind
just like my tears
never made a difference

<u>dead things.</u>

poetry is a graveyard
for all of the people
who hurt me

punishment.

you were the cancer
in my heart
punishing me for feeling
so deeply

several sessions.

it begins to fail
and so we think
try harder
make changes
do more

we call on the attention
of therapists
to provide emotional therapy
to whatever has broken
within that relationship
pumping our hard-earned money
into fixing something
that feels even more broken
after each session

the drive home
gets longer
silence fills the car
there's no longer room
for peace, the tension
has taken over
and there's no denying
this truth

it has already failed
and so we think
we're not trying hard enough
doing more
just makes it worse

not every relationship
deserves this type of energy
not every relationship
can be saved with therapy

fought for.

you've always been
the only one making an effort
it's time someone fought for you

a human condition.

i've been guilty
of giving advice
that i'd struggle
to follow

in common.

cheaters think
everyone is unfaithful
liars think
no one tells the truth
keep this in mind

what people think of others
may actually tell you more
about themselves

missing may.

i used to volunteer at retirement
homes

i've always believed that i could
learn more

from spending time with people who
had

actually lived their lives

old age grants wisdom in most cases

and there was always a lesson

to be learned from someone

who was much older than me

i'll never forget this one
conversation

i had with a woman who was well

into her 80s

she'd tell me how lonely life was

or how painful it had become

facing the realization that she'd

never known unconditional love

she'd never gotten married

and she didn't have any children

she said that she thought

she'd always have time

all the parties

all the temporary fun

the memories she created

that would later mean nothing

as she sat alone near the window

in her wheelchair

looking at life outside

hoping for another chance

that she'd never get

she enjoyed sex and so she

took many lovers who never loved her

the one relationship she had

was unhealthy

a cancer to her life and she never

wanted kids because she thought

they would slow her down

because to her, life was only a
party

nothing more than bars and clubs

loud music and drinks

strangers pretending to care

just to get what they wanted

but she was young then and she
thought

she had time

she looked at me with tears in her
eyes

and said

i wasted my time

and now there's nothing left

she died a few days later

and that conversation changed my
life

in fact, the conversations i've had

with people nearing the end of
their lives

have really changed the way i live
my own

do something now

that your future will appreciate

the loudest silence.

maybe it's actually
not that serious
maybe i simply
care too much
maybe you're so used
to having a partner
who never cares for you
maybe having someone like me
is too overwhelming for you

i think this is how i learned
to stop giving a fuck
i went cold, i became numb
this is how i learned
to fall short of feeling
for people incapable
of appreciating me

not easy.

sleep rarely comes easy

for the souls who linger

overthinking about overthinking

the playback of past events

haunted by the memories

of someone or something

possibly a choice, a regret

or desire to relive a mistake

in an effort to right their wrongs

those chances are non-existent

and so we struggle to live with our
past

while trying to live in the moment

sleep never comes easy

all knowing soul.

when a woman is constantly hurt

she sees things for what they truly
are

she's heard it all before

you can sell your dreams

and tell your lies

but deep down she knows

nightmare 2010.

i believe that loving

the wrong person

is like experiencing a nightmare

that you can't wake up from

until you've arrived at the
realization

that loving someone

won't always make them love you back

this relationship.

if your loyalty isn't appreciated
it's okay to walk away
loving someone means
remaining by their side
but there's only so much
you can do with someone
who isn't mature enough
to understand your true value

no sacrifice.

stop sacrificing yourself
and your happiness for love

real love will never
require you to do so

womankind.

women are truly amazing
and i feel as though the good ones
never truly receive the credit
they deserve
from relationship stress
dealing with insecurities
cramps and the responsibility
of carrying the future of mankind
in their womb for 9 months

a woman's pain tolerance
is unmatched
her patience is legendary
she loves hard and her loyalty
is remarkable

i appreciate the female gender
the good, the strong women
thank you for adding value
to this world
i'm sure it's not easy
but somehow you manage to smile
and remain strong

chains.

never allow your loyalty
to become a form of slavery
your loyalty means nothing
to someone who isn't mature
enough to honor it

it's okay to move on
sweetheart, set yourself free

transitions.

being loyal to someone
who doesn't appreciate it
is wasted energy

loving someone who treats
you like you're ordinary
is a waste of emotion

a moment spent
thinking about the people
who never consider how you feel
is a waste of time

sometimes walking away
gives you an opportunity to run
into someone who will support
your desire to be happy

hear silence.

even with a closed mouth
a woman can express so much
with her silence

you decided.

you're single by choice
understanding what it means
to be taken for granted
you've promised yourself
to never settle again

facts of life.

life taught me
that the people
you're most loyal to
will often be the ones
to screw you over
in the cruelest of ways

f.t.i.

fuck this idea of staying
after being cheated on
simply because you love that person
and start embracing the fact that you
can do better

out of anger.

never trust your tongue
when your heart is angry

testing patience.

she won't give up on you easily
but that doesn't mean you should see
how far you can go
before she's finally gone

no bullshit.

they call her crazy
they say she's angry
they claim she's bipolar
or maybe moody
simply because she's decided
to no longer put up
with the bullshit that plagues
most relationships

requirement I.

all she wants is someone
who wants her just as much
as she wants them
what she requires is the truth
all she deserves is loyalty
that's not asking for too much

requirement II.

so many women are single
by choice because it's better
to be alone than in a relationship
with someone who
isn't mature enough to provide
the type of treatment
a good woman requires

attentive.

she values attentiveness
a woman can tell a lot about a man
who devotes his attention to her

key.

never do something
that you'll feel the need
to hide from your
significant other

this is what i learned
this is what has saved me

awakened.

one day his apologies
will hold no meaning
one day you'll no longer
feel the urge to give them
a second chance
and you'll give them silence
because you'll understand
that they no longer
deserve your words

together we fix.

my heart is open
after being closed
while with someone
who promised to keep it
time alters what's familiar
people change
you couldn't see it
hesitant to love again
but even so, my heart is open
you've felt what i felt
so let's fall and together
we'll fix what was broken

no re-entry.

they leave you for "someone better"
that someone turns out to be
a waste of time
when they come back to you
say no

tell them you can do better

every lesson.

learn from a failed relationship

learn from what you had

so that you can have

what you deserve in terms

of future relationships

do it now.

go wherever you want
as far as you want
whenever you want
there is no time
like now
there is no time
like the present

a lifetime.

i want the sadness

that comes with the ending

of something everlasting

i want the pain

that follows losing my best friend

i deserve a love

that is so profound and powerful

that when lost

i lose myself entirely

within that moment

i deserve a love

that can only end

with death

overwhelmed overcoming.

the tip of the empire state building
hides behind a deep fog
the sky, gloomy
setting the mood for sadness
the raindrops silently tap the window
the raindrops slightly paint the city
some with umbrellas
those who came prepared
many without
many people unaware
but the beauty of it all
that no matter what the weather
no matter how much
or how often the rain falls
the people do not stop
the people keep going
you must keep going

going forward.

be with someone
who doesn't force you
to compete with everything else
in their lives

who you are.

you are simply

a lifetime of moments

a bundle of flaws

a bag of magic

an existence full of purpose

a heart filled with love

you are to be experienced

within you lives profound meaning

within you lives endless possibilities

save all of this

all of you, for someone

who will appreciate you entirely

refusal.

this should have never gone this far

we should have never gotten to this place

here in this moment, together

destined to fail, blinded by denial

gripping hold to false hope

this was never a love story

just a nightmare

we refused to wake up from

you decide.

it's always the people

closest to you

the ones you tell

your secrets to

the men you trust

the women you confide in

the individuals

you'd do anything for

these people

are your biggest investments

these people

are the keepers of

your secrets

the ones you look to

for protection and love

yet these are the same people

who hold the power

to destroy you in ways

you'd never imagine

be careful who

you give that power to

1989.

my story begins there

love sitting on fragile wings

a future of happiness denied

by one's decision

to be led by their heart

while deciding to ignore their
instincts

my mother chose him

i didn't and i guess there's

a part of me that will always
question

her choices when it comes to my father

maybe she was charmed by his lies

a moment of deceit, hidden behind his
smile

the way he elegantly danced around

his true intentions for marrying her

whatever it was or could've been

here i am, writing this to you

spilling out my inconvenient and
painful truths

with this hope that you'll

find something meaningful

sitting within these pages

my initial existence

all based upon a man's triumph

in fooling some beautiful soul

into thinking he actually cared for her

a realization that has haunted me

ever since i could actually

muster up a memory

archives.

my poetry is an archive
of heartache and disappointment

flow.

let your tears become the river
that washes away your pain

self-serve.

your soul knows
how to heal itself
maybe in being alone
you have all you'll need

several summers.

you broke me down
you ruined my ideology of love
and so the only sane thing to do
was to go mad
i lost my mind
i lost myself

altered states.

you used to know me
my identity altered
by the reality of investing
my love into the wrong lover

route.

happiness waits around the corner
knowing when to turn is our issue

rock bottom.

i tried to be an anchor
for the both of us
and nearly drowned

nearly 5 a.m.

all my demons
came in the form of love
deceitful little things
proclaiming a love
that turned out to be untrue

wrong script.

i've tried writing our love story
in a script made for a horror film
you were my hell
and yet i searched for heaven in you

a way out.

the same strength
used to hold on
is the same strength
i used to let go

wind chill.

the very thought of you
brings about winter
in my chest

missing me.

sometimes i struggle
with the idea of being missed
incapable of imagining myself, me
as an individual that people
actually think about
and i guess that in itself
says a lot about the way
i view myself

your own.

there will come a moment
within your life
where you'll have to accept the fact
that right now you're on your own
and the only one who will save you
is yourself

the evolution of sadness.

little sad girls

learn to master

their strength so early

young sad girls

evolve into powerful women

me against me.

my mind, my heart
the endless argument
of what i know and what i feel
two major pieces of me
at odds and in battle
fighting for my attention
longing for my validation

each day.

always thinking
mind stirring
incapable of stopping
the day comes in flashes
bleeding into the night
i fade into myself
like the sun behind the horizon
of the sea
unable to sleep
even while the darkness of the night
covers me

the untrue.

how many people
have written
their names on your heart
with empty promises of forever
and proclamations that meant nothing

a modern struggle.

it's hard not knowing
how to not want the person
who oftentimes
reveals shades of someone
you shouldn't be with

there is struggle
there is confusion
there is grief

the girls who read.

i know that you sit weary
next to the window
listening to the rain
reading books about how
you'd wish your life was
daydreaming about being
the type of girl
that poets write about
trying to escape the madness
that has become your life

i wrote this about you

deep and dire.

my mornings are swollen
bruised by my insomnia
made weak by my restlessness
the struggle of finding sleep
while nursing these emotional wounds

it pains me.

the painful reality
of being stuck in a place
beside a stranger
who used to feel
like love

just some.

some people
are versions of hell
we never thought
we'd experience

5:07 a.m.

go slowly
be patient
with the woman
who is used to heartbreak

5:08 a.m.

let pain teach you
if it hurts
it's a lesson

5:09 a.m.

weakness

no longer knows

her name

5:10 a.m.

look deep within yourself
for any and everything
you've been missing

5:11 a.m.

i stopped holding on to you
i am in desperate need of myself

5:13 a.m.

the flowers in my garden

envy women like you

5:14 a.m.

bury your past like seeds
grow a new garden
with deeper roots
and stronger roses

hear her.

a woman naked
bare to the world
covered in stories
worth reading out loud
worth listening to

5:17 a.m.

do not give your whole
to those who are only willing
to love you half the time

the root of it all.

they only see your flower
and so they compliment
  the surface
but i admire your roots

5:20 a.m.

stop
allow no one the option
of treating you like a secret
do you not realize
that a heart like yours
should be loved out loud
in front of the world
to see

13 hours ago.

look deep within your own heart
for everything you are missing

shipwreck.

you can't keep
what shouldn't stay
you can't anchor
a shipwreck

beauty still remains.

she is full of wounds
riddled with scars
but she is still standing
and she is still beautiful

vowing unhappiness.

you know what saddens my soul
watching people remain in chains
to a mate who is no longer willing
to appreciate their love
two people who took vows
that are no longer meaningful
while only holding on to each other
because divorce is too expensive
this is not love, it's prison

where i hid.

you helped me get lost
you were once
my favorite hiding place

6:25 p.m.

struggling to be sober
i am almost clean of you

6:27 p.m.

you were winter

when i preferred warmth

6:29 p.m.

if bruises could speak

they'd tell stories

of pain inflicted

by those who pretended

to love us

just thinking.

i wish i could stretch
out time
and put more of you
in it

<u>from mother.</u>

she had her mother's patience
the gift of understanding
the curse of holding on
too long

to someone like you.

this is for the girls

who remain quiet

hurting in silence

screaming without words

i feel you

i see you

i hear you

forecast.

chase the storm
inside her soul

that emptiness.

i was drowning
in the echo
of your empty
promises

a home in you.

i just wanted you
to speak to me
for so long
your voice felt like home

6:36 p.m.

perhaps my love story
no longer exists in you

near the moon.

of all the stars
sitting in the night sky
you are the brightest
do not hide your light

inside.

she carries the future
in her womb

21st day of January.

encouraging women
is not the equivalent
of hating men

6:55 p.m.

the part of me
that continued
chasing you
has decided
to walk away
toward something
better

7:01 p.m.

all this time

i've been searching

for someone

who would accept

and appreciate my flaws

each of you.

every woman
has a story within her
too big for the mind
of weak men
to comprehend

7:55 p.m.

let him miss you

let him regret

forcing you away

let him see you happy

but never let him back in

7:57 p.m.

her love was too tall
out of reach
and too large to be held
by unworthy hands

always smiling.

her eyes were sad
her heart was broken
and her mind, overwhelmed
but she smiled

dark waltz.

i am guilty of
searching for heaven
while dancing with devils

reflect me.

i stopped searching
for myself in mirrors
i found my reflection
in you

8:06 p.m.

goodbyes are knives
i've cut so many

one evening.

no warning

no farewells

no words

just silence

we met our end

on an unexpected

evening

changes everything.

if that one day
where that one thing
never happened
everything would be
so different right now

ask yourself.

think of this moment
as your last
think of the ending of it all
arriving soon

are you satisfied
with your life
are you content
with your relationship
have you loved someone
capable of loving you back
have you known a love
that doesn't compromise your joy
are you with someone
who deserves your heart

if this was it
the end and nothing more
are you happy with
what you've had

here by myself.

somewhere a long time ago
i left behind all of the things
that made me hopeful and happy
just to make room for more of you

this was my mistake
this would later become
my biggest regret
losing me entirely
just to keep you here

failing to realize
that true love would never
force me to compromise
or abandon the things
that brought me peace

say no, say yes.

i stand by this idea that life
doesn't have to be some
complex ordeal
life doesn't have to be
some long drawn out mess
a roller coaster
of fucked up things
and events that ruin
the quality of living

life doesn't have to be
a version of hell
it doesn't have to be filled
with pain

the story of your life

is a choice

and it's time to choose yourself

it's time to look in the mirror

and see the strength in your
reflection

it's time to protect your heart

and soul from the hands

of abusers and those looking

to bring harm

right now

here in this moment

is an opportunity

to find what you've lost

and to retrieve what is truly yours

say no

to what hurts you

say yes

to what heals you

maid.

relationships, marriages

two people working together

not one person, working

under the other

a mate should never feel

like a maid in their relationship

unhappy, unhealthy.

marriage doesn't always
equate to love
those rings mean nothing
without peace
effort, loyalty, support,
and communication

man child.

how sad
watching a woman
become a wife
as well as a mother
to her husband
who instead of being a man
chooses to act like a child

i'm listening.

her emotions are the loudest
when she's silent

modern battle.

i found myself competing
with your phone
reaching for you
while you were reaching for it

disconnection I.

we started to become those people
we said we'd never be
hours on hours spent together
but not actually together
sitting next to each other
but never present
our phones were distractions
they caused our disconnect

disconnection II.

there's something about cell phones
that create a total disconnect
between two people. sadly, they
become distractions. destroying
bonds and communication. i've
always hated the feeling of being
neglected or ignored by someone
who would rather look at a screen
instead of me. sitting in silence
as they scroll through the photos
of strangers instead of speaking to
me. people would rather hold their
mobile devices instead of holding
on to those who truly care for
them. only realizing that they've
been neglectful when it's entirely
too late. finally looking up from
their phone and the person who sat
patiently waiting is no longer there.
as much as i enjoy social media, i
hate that it can often destroy the
social aspect of a relationship.

the thought of it.

i've been thinking about walking
away from you for a very long time.
i've been dancing around the idea of
removing you from my life entirely.
i've grown closer to what i deserve
which means i'm growing further
from you, and that thought no longer
bothers me. no longer restricted by
my fears of losing you, i've finally
realized that you could never be lost
and that realization is my fucking
freedom.

unforgiving I.

never hurt the heart of someone
who loves you unconditionally
people who love deeply
can be so fucking unforgiving
and cold when their love and warmth
isn't appreciated

unforgiving II.

it takes so much fucking courage
to feel love and i was brave enough
to express it to you. maybe that's
why i'm so cold, empty, entirely
drained from giving my best to
someone who decided that it was not
enough. maybe i'm so unforgiving
because i gave to you entirely, my
truth and compassion. my time and
energy. all of that to be made to
feel like i was nothing in the end.
the more you love, the more you hate
it. the more you give, the more they
take, and this is why i can walk
away from you without a care in the
world. knowing that i tried for you
will always be a regret that i'll
live with but i'll find peace in
knowing that i buried you beneath
my feet then walked away toward
something better with someone
better.

knowing myself.

i've been labeled cocky, a simple
misunderstanding and misprint
describing my entire personality. all
based upon the fact that i'm aware
of my self-worth. knowing that anyone
would be hard pressed or completely
stressed out trying to search for
someone else like me. this is my power,
being able to do what most refuse to.
how easily i'm considered different
from anything or everything you've
grown used to. so when i say, "you'll
regret losing me" understand this is
not meant to be threatening or an act
of wishing bad upon your life. it's
the understanding that what i am
and who i am is considered something
rare. everything about me, from the
way i think to the way i carry on
about life or within my relationship is
something that is often desired, rarely
appreciated and hardest to obtain. i am
the soul regret of those who couldn't
keep me due to neglect and lies. i am
the greatest loss to those who thought
i could easily be replaced. i am the
constant reminder of what they could
have had. this itself is powerful, this
in itself makes me powerful. knowing
myself, knowing my truth.

promise this to self.

i made a promise that i would never
allow myself to feel like i've felt
in the past. unappreciated, taken
for granted and betrayed by the
words of someone who claimed to have
loved me. tired of the soul-draining
task of trying for someone who never
actually cared. i've continued to
walk through life, walking away
without regret. never willing to
stay in a space with someone who
made me feel like i was nothing or
no one. i've been love deprived for
so long that being alone became my
heaven and being cold was a form of
solitude. there is a piece of bliss
within the realization of self-value
and there is peace in burying anyone
who has made you feel like you were
never good enough for them to love
and so i've dug many holes for the
souls of lovers who fell short of
loving me and this will always be my
power, knowing when to fight, when
to stay and when walking away means
being closer to a lover who will
never break my heart.

find this, keep this.

if you should ever find love in a
relationship with someone who sees
beauty in your imperfections and
potential in your shortcomings,
hold on to them. they are the
people who want love. the people
who will reciprocate the love
of those willing to give and
then there are people who have
hearts that are made of stone and
a smile that will turn into an
empty expression of lies in the
end. unconditional love is a lost
art and those who know it and are
willing to give it deserve someone
who will be ready and willing to
give them the same effort and
energy. do not stay where you
are no longer appreciated and do
not go to where your presence or
absence will not be acknowledged
or felt. love thy self then love
someone capable of loving you
entirely.

too many illusions.

you're living comfortably in an
illusion. your friendships, illusions.
your relationship, an illusion. your
marriage, a giant illusion. lies that
you've chosen to believe. giving off
the scent of perfection while rotting
away with time, hidden behind this
image of what you think your life
should be. you live in this perfect
picture, suppressing your reality,
ignoring your truth. this is hurting
you, pretending to be happy is hard
work and it's draining you. your
inability to want more has kept you in
a situation that continues to rob you
of your joy. the things that you've
chosen to accept have been destroying
your peace. hell hidden behind a
smile. deceit hidden behind, "i love
you." you've grown comfortable with no
growth, no progression. things will
never get better until you realize
that you deserve better.

after midnight in 2009.

your phone went off after 2 a.m.
and i'd happened to be up,
restlessness filling my soul as
i allowed my curiosity to get the
best of me. i reached over you to
retrieve your phone, with this idea
that maybe this notification would
lead me to an emergency from either
one of your friends or possibly
family but it didn't. i could feel
my own heart sink deeper within
my chest, positioning itself in
a way that made me feel so damn
uncomfortable. i will never tell
you what i read. i won't even tell
you that i did this. i read the
message plenty times over then
deleted it, but what was felt will
be something i'll never forget and
you'll never be able to apologize
or make me feel better about it
because i'll never give you the
opportunity to feed me a lie in
an effort to make me feel better
about it.

i'm still fighting.

i'm afraid that i won't make it
out of this. constantly living in
my head, haunted by my thoughts.
this endless cycle of overthinking,
losing myself in the dark. trying to
surrender to the moon but unable to
find sleep. these are my nightmares,
the terrors in the night that i
often face head on, wide awake, eyes
open. witnessing the unraveling of
myself as if i was looking into
a mirror, staring in horror of my
own reflection. i'm afraid but i am
brave, still willing to fight for my
peace of mind.

angry women.

an angry woman
is powerful
an angry woman
makes history
an angry woman
destroys barriers
an angry woman
is beautiful

without explaining why.

to be completely honest, i've never
actually been good at staying. i've
mastered the art of changing my mind
about people pretty easily. silently
walking away from anyone who no longer
benefits my journey toward happiness.
i want to make connections with others
but my need to be alone has always
outweighed my desire for companionship
or friendship. there's this high in the
realization and/or knowing that you
never truly need another person but
you allow them to share a space in your
life because you simply care for them,
but so often in my own life, people
have continued to let me down and it's
because of this that i've continued to
walk away without regret. without any
explanation.

the thick of it.

the fantasy of it all is so much
better than the reality of
everything. we daydream for hours,
hiding from the struggles of
everyday life. we paint over the
cracks in the wall with enough
bullshit to keep us mentally
sedated. we spend so much time
running from emotion instead of
standing tall in the face of every
breakdown. it is important to
know that falling apart is never
permanent and sometimes falling
down gives us the opportunity to be
built back up, much stronger than
before.

soul break.

they always talk about the heart
breaking but no one mentions the
soul and how much of a beating it
takes when trying to move on with
life after being hit with emotional
trauma. i don't know about everyone
else but sometimes, it's not just
the heart that breaks. i myself have
many cracks in my soul and wounds
that still hurt.

first of first.

our first loves
were our first
heartbreaks

ready.

we waited
i loved her
before i touched her
i committed to her entirely
before i touched her physically
we didn't make love
until we cultivated love
outside of the bedroom
and when we were ready
her flower bloomed for me

within me.

this is what i did differently
i didn't go searching for love
i looked within myself
for everything my exes
refused to give me
and i realized that the things
i could never get were always
living within my own heart

orevwa.

emotions trapped inside a screen
making things harder to read
so much frustration in my soul
out of control, i want to scream

text messages or emails
i call, you never answer
these phones are no help
cell phones are like cancer

no more face to face
we're not seeing eye to eye
you can't see my painful stare
you don't see my teary eyes

somewhere sitting by the phone
somewhere dark, all alone
somehow the pain is so deep
because i feel it in my bones

and my soul is no better
i'll say i'm fine but i'm not
a victim to anxiety
right now my stomach is in knots

but you don't even care
you're never there
you never were

i'm sorry
i miss you
just a string of empty words

so here's my last reply
my emotions in a text
i'm afraid, full of fear
because i don't know what's next

you can respond if you'd like
but at this point
it doesn't matter

see i'm searching
for clarity
and you're no longer
the one i'm after

the end . . .

index.

planting gardens in graves III

Andrews McMeel Publishing
a division of Andrews McMeel Universal
1130 Walnut Street, Kansas City, Missouri 64106

www.andrewsmcmeel.com

18 19 20 21 22 RR2 10 9 8 7 6 5 4 3 2 1

ISBN: 978-1-4494-8944-1

Library of Congress Control Number: 2018940696

Editor: Patty Rice

Art Director, Designer: Diane Marsh

Production Editor: David Shaw

Production Manager: Cliff Koehler

attention: schools and businesses

Andrews McMeel books are available at
quantity discounts with bulk purchase for
educational, business, or sales promotional
use. For information, please e-mail the Andrews
McMeel Publishing Special Sales Department:
specialsales@amuniversal.com.